IDEAS 1

OR

THE IMPERATIVE BOOK 1

RC PATTERSON

Copyright © 2013 RC Patterson

All rights reserved.

Dogma

The problem I raise here is not what ought to succeed mankind in the sequence of species (the human being is a conclusion): but what type of human being one ought to breed, ought to will, as more valuable, more worthy of life, more certain of the future............................ (Nietzsche)

RC Patterson

Dogma

Idea's 1

(Or,
The Imperative Book 1)

RC Patterson

Dogma

Psychological

Part 1
Section 1
1

Selected characteristic
Is 18 to 24
The highest in poverty
Guess it means nothing mother roared
Echoes cascade to my cave from the door
Upstairs she's in pain
Ringing the call to care
I never went my sister did
She helps carry the family til she's blistered its
The 29.9 percent
Making well under thirty five thousand
In my mind I lament
But survival means being entitled
What do you expect with poverty?
Constant at 24 point whatever percent
I know you don't expect a words smith
Writing about my findings
Underground trying to converse with
Melodic tong sounds, I heard his
Steps into my life world, I got nervous
The voice said "do my will"
I was out of time
Maybe we could talk about why
But I was raised to be stout, to whine
Or discuss issues is a personal crime
The only thing worst is to cry
So I blamed him for my problem

RC Patterson

And I said "let me be"
Into my cave
Came a reconstruction
And my reckoning
His return
Meant my exit

Poverty is a problem we all face reluctantly
The urban authors failed, gluttons lead
We, the progeny of the Right, bleed out
Ignored by gods, we are in dire need

Poverty is a problem we all face reluctantly
The urban authors failed, gluttons lead
We, the progeny of the Right, bleed out

The progeny of the Right

The progeny of the old Right

Dogma

2

Now imagine a community gated
By a street
Inside was the lunacy of unsated
Lives in heat
In winter the 34 percent
Will freeze
Unsupervised lurking
In the street
I walk past them as they
Talk of the tragic workings
Of the elites
Because some grow up fast
Others learn to love only what's fast
The streets shine
On dreams lost in time
Sweaty kids try to be ballers
Ready with passion
In a desert
I happened past a lesser
God's specter
I looked at the pressure
The stress under her eyes
I wondered what
Could give her those bags, her strife
Must have stunted her like
A lightning strike
To leave her like
A fallen once mighty pine
Up against the black gate
I have pain in my head

I need
Something to crush it
So I take
Some acetaminophen
On an empty stomach
Now the nausea makes
Me feel like rubbish
I look at the disparity
And wonder
How one could love it
There in these structures
Brick skinned mothers
Live in utter
Misery, but it's a wonder
How their strength
Remains tough

Poverty is a problem we all face reluctantly
The urban authors failed, gluttons lead
We, the progeny of the Right, bleed out
Ignored by gods, we are in dire need

Poverty is a problem we all face reluctantly
The urban authors failed, gluttons lead
We, the progeny of the Right, bleed out

The progeny of the Right

The progeny of the old Right

Dogma

I remember going
To the grocery store
The Aldis
I saw some obese girl with palsy
Angry at the right I set face
Wondering what kind of sorcery could abort
All opportunity
In little over a decade
The more I see these beings
I question the divinities
A man tries
To sell me some EBT
I told him no
Like I tell those homeless with fat lies
Who say they need to eat
"Look I'll buy you some food"
They answer never mind
And that's why I'm mistrustful
But still give to some, blue
Sky turns dark gray
Up high is natures
Art, paint is gray dust
We are destined to become
Sometimes I walk merely
To think up reasons
For me to be here
The urban is yellow
Wallpaper and her people
Are dreams
Mere scenes in a sad
Reality near me
They walk, the dead zombies

I run to the court of the dragon
They gain speed mocking me
I awake thinking "what happened?"
I fell asleep
In my cave, in the dream
Anguish drove me mad
I fell asleep in my lament
That's all I think about
The massacring
Slaughter of poverty
Because that pain is
My life water
In an instant all
Goes black "am I slipping," got
A message from a voice behind me
"You are now in the hands of the living God"

Dogma

Part 1
Section 2
1

A company of
Explorer conquers
Tourists looking for
The origin that
Receptacle of deep
Knowing the
Perpetual Eidolon
I was looking from a window sill
At the symbols grilled
On his regalia
The leader looks
Back at his pale lot
One speaks up
But is pushed back by
The cadence of the leader
"We were placed here for a reason"
He said without disdain
Meanings permeate their faces
Anger seethes as they search for the displaced
No humans are outside
To guide them
Through the ruins
Abandoned shrines and homesteads
One soldier see's something moving
A few rush toward it
But it's just some old vet
Begging, poor old dreg
Before they left him he said
"Welcome to the dead city"

They should have left
Then it hit me
They will never leave
I pick up leather seams
Left by those whose
Armor is too heavy
Many of them begin dropping shields
As they begin to realize they
Are in the desert of the real
Food desert
Bloated soldiers starve as the
Sun turns them dark
The leader merely
Walks ahead, they toil in the dirt and starve
Many consider mutiny
Cut off from resources
Anger burns in their hearts

The first now the last
Forever feels his two-ness
An un-reconciled vat
The impromptu integration was foolish
Marginality and alienation is so grueling

It happened to fast

The first now the last
Forever feels his two-ness
An un-reconciled vat
It happened to fast

Dogma

2

Decades pass the centurion
Kills off the transformed with scurvy tricks
The mutiny was sacked, it took too long
With no throng to mask me
I picked up a gold clad piece
Of armor, he had seen
The marker
Of the chosen on my arm
Like dark paint
He said "you are stained
I need a guide
Before I embark again"
I told him I would show him
Where his trophy remains
If he pays
With something deep he agreed
And acquiesced to the condition
That my prize will be on a
Need be basis given
We came upon an
Elaborate labyrinth
That had the scent
Of something antediluvian
We traveled well into the enigma
When we neared the center, I picked up
Some speed and cleared his vision, he went up
Farther, angry, in fear, sick of
The dark seeing a light
Around a corner
He scurried forth seeing the Eidolon
Before e him little did he know it was

RC Patterson

Me, he said "it must be a mistake
I would have known"
"Seppi" I said, "it's a dream
Your ideals and beliefs
Are falsely based
On the real
Through faulty claims
Now you wonder what
I'm demanding
All I want from you
Is understanding."

The first now the last
Forever feels his two-ness
An un-reconciled vat
The impromptu integration was foolish
Marginality and alienation is so grueling

It happened to fast

The first now the last
Forever feels his two-ness
An un-reconciled vat
It happened to fast

It happened to fast

Dogma

So don't question me
Leader of the Mysteries
I taught the Greeks
Check your history
Now you're mad to see
Me and my Negros'
On the bas-relief
Teaching Greeks
There on that ship
Stands Heraclitus

RC Patterson

Part 1
Section 3
1

The street is a barrior
A sign of the defeat
Beware of the mines
Placed there, the heat
Is unbearable as
I stare at the neat
Fortresses, castles
Of the fairest of kings
Is what his title is
Listed in his liablest
Bibles which he gives
To our schools to eat
Because he bared food
From the breed to starve out
Our overmen
Because we don't admit
We quarter them
Water kid seeds
Who grow into rebel trees
No more rebel reeds
Crushed by his
Grinder
Into papyrus
We are wise
To your stone thinking
And your lying forgers
Your Simoninis'
But he's still after me, a pawn
A demon spawn

Dogma

Trying to
Capture me or kill me
Is it my soul he wants?
To steal, bleak vistas' await me
In the lake we
Must make each
Other into prey
Because there is no escape, kings
Have set up traps
For lessor beings that
They don't need and
Don't want to see
The right is undaunted
By the scene
Of wanton poverty
Left to fester
Next to lavishly incrusted effects
Means and realties
Hiding behind some ruble
I see my double
The dark
Wilson with the stubble
On his chin

The Imperative said
Beware of his steps

The fact is knowing
That fighting back ain't hopeless

RC Patterson

Let's rupture this system
That has lead nations
Into structures of segregation

The Imperative said
Beware of his steps

Let's rupture this system

2

The Imperative said
Beware of his steps
The god killer
You can't stop, he'll turn
Demi gods into
Fileted bones
With the sword of Cratos
It was the integration
That disintegrated
The hope
In this matrix
He was surveying
A corner
I murked him
With some hard wood
His head hit the pavement
I ran back to my basement
Thinking of the storm
But I sit on a foundation
Where I've found great wisdom
In eruditions
That grounds my inheritance
I look in the mirror
And there it is
The ambition
Of the Imperative
And the mission
Given to me by she
The true fair one, with
The understanding
And explosive verse

I will destroy the walls
And remand
The lords of my peoples curse
Those who will not
Dismantle the walls
The treacherous
Numen will fall
The crab that's stocked
In a barrel
And never allowed to exit
Will develop certain
Characteristics
Lessons burned in
The creature adapts to his
Hindrance
By devouring those people
He meets in many instances
It was simple, a matter
Of my intention
That my double found me
He said "the murders will end with
Your decent in to prison."
I answered "you've bound me
Not what I have written."

The Imperative said

Let's rupture this system

The fact is knowing
That fighting back ain't hopeless

Dogma

Fighting back ain't hopeless

Let's rupture this system
That has lead nations
Into structures of segregation

Fighting back ain't hopeless

Let's rupture this system

Fighting back ain't hopeless

Part 1
Section 4
1

I am the extraordinary man
Next to lord this very black
City, if he isn't with she then he's
Minced meat
Simply survival
In bleak recitals, needs chime
Through lean minds who see why
Criminal fists are individualist
Changing society with sinful hits
To moral tables from old times
Based on poor old fables, sold minds
Can't be brought back, only shattered
Moldy splatters of quotes in attics
Up ladders of the psyche
Where the father is buried
I think their dreams
Can be designed by me
As I bind dying streets
By uniting breed
In an alliance of holy beings
While defying the police
The higher man killed two sisters
Let him die
Or establish a new truth with her
Power, my loud curse
Drowns out foul verse
In Razumihin's apartment,
A change from yellow, we sit
Discussing darkness

Dogma

As a political tool to spark this
Revolution I spoke the theory
In third person so Porfiry
Wouldn't suspect my new truth

I am the extraordinary man
Next to lord this very black
City, if he isn't with she then he's

I am the extraordinary man
Next to lord this very black
City, if he isn't with she then he's

I am the extraordinary man
Next to lord this very black
City, if he isn't with she then he's minced meat

I am the extraordinary man

I am the extraordinary
No cruelty, no feast

I am the extraordinary
No cruelty, no feast

2

In theory clearly
I would have had
To kill Porfiry
The poor dearie
With a cord nearly
Severing his head
From the torso
Leaving bleeding arteries, for those
Who question my martyring your own
I left Razuminhin's dwellings
For Mr. Wildes settlings
"You need this"
He tells me
A book with worn files
The files were a manuscript
And manifesto
Of the means
We must use
And the line
In the dynasty
The text was the Imperative
Not the King
In Yellow
I couldn't believe it
Every time I read it
"Well, you will lead," he said
I answered "me"
"This fellow
Will assist us
With our plans"
He said "the dupe,"

Dogma

Was fearfully in accord
Vance
Was his name
Once insane
Like me an individual
In the herd
The end game you see
Hinges on my word
I grew up to stupid too
Weak to fight
Turned my head
In this cave to find her
She the ethereal
Is it my time
She said "it's nearing you"
I was a victim
Of situation
Until I claimed
My slave ship

I am the extraordinary man
Next to lord this very black
City, if he isn't with she then he's

I am the extraordinary man
Next to lord this very black
City, if he isn't with she then he's

I am the extraordinary man
Next to lord this very black
City, if he isn't with she then he's minced meat

I am the extraordinary man

I am the extraordinary
No cruelty, no feast

I am the extraordinary
No cruelty, no feast

No cruelty, no feast

No cruelty, no feast

No cruelty, no feast

Dogma

Transcendental
Part 2
Section 1
1

Not merely a lack
Of what we all need
The essence of poverty
Is inequality
Conservative theoreticians
Blame those born in this
World with slim
Chances, they act
Anti-economically
To the right ecology
In every society
Should consider the future
Or die, texts speak
Of the culture of poverty
As a hopeless oddity
Using jokes
About welfare folks
To produce mockery
By the time kids are
Six or seven
They absorb the basic values
And are given poor lessons
To conservatives
These children are hopeless
Stupid soulless kids with
One penchant
Steeped in criminal goals it is
The capitalist system

That has to produce victims
A reserve army
Of unemployed women
And children
For the sake of keeping
Wages low
Decisions made by those
In the pangs of old
Structural chains
Are limited to the
Barriers
Places there deep
Left in defacto
Patterns rarely do
The people vote
Or watch the dispatch
News
No politics beyond
Family views

Lifestyles on bad streets is paternized
Choken out dreams are shattered, eyes
See faded beings happen by

The most hated
The most hated

Lifestyles on bad streets is paternized
Choken out dreams are shattered, eyes
See faded beings happen by

The most hated
The most hated

Part 2
Section 1
2

The clustered poor
Attracts the same
Economic strain
They agglomerate
Poverty
Locked in space
Places indoctrinate
Toddlers, dreams
Of kings
Migrate
From the island
While the magician
Spins the cycle
And the right says
That's purely
Their decision
The cycle
Repeats itself
At an individual level
The spiral
Of disinvestment
A cyclical hex, closed
Liquor and retail stores
Due to a lack of
Community tethers, ropes
Sit too high to reach
Students can't get those
Books they need to read
Through the fires

Of ritual life worlds
Sick and tired
Of race making sites for
Firms the lack of skilled labor
Means cutting edge
Technology
Isn't built in those chambers
And if they are
They don't use regional labor
People fail to invest
In their children's future

Lifestyles on bad streets is paternized
Choken out dreams are shattered, eyes
See faded beings happen by

The most hated
The most hated

Lifestyles on bad streets is paternized
Choken out dreams are shattered, eyes
See faded beings happen by

The most hated
The most hated

Dogma

Part 2
Section 2
1

Due to social history
Changes
Debates about a
Genetic foundation of
Race
Are unsound the claims
Are
Attempts to ground race
In physiological bounds, chains
It's an attempt
To justify poverty
Rich men are thus
The right lot to lead
The masses of inferior
Detractors of his mirror, war
Against him is futile, lords
Among men rule styles born
Of them who now, beg them
For mercy and food while hordes
Starve, he's quenched
But the darker
Ruled before
The lighter order
The darkness marks us
A fear of change
And the other
Steered the hate
And the need to
Discriminate

Our brothers
And sisters

The intellegensia has failed to limit us
Nationalism is an irationalism

The intellegensia has failed to limit us

The intellegensia has failed to limit us

2

Blood stains
Their ancestry
And their being has
Been formulated through
Racialization a groups
Cultural imperatives
Compel rational
Behavioral
Decisions their intent
Is survival
The rights to vain to see
That is why
We deviate from
The mainstream
That most naïve
Egoism
Fascist irrationalism
Instincts that carry over from
Life habits of the
Dim past
Seek refuge
In nationalism
The authoritarian
Attempts to enact
Pure barriers
Through intra group contact
In America racism
Was used to create
A labor class
Separation of groups
By race

RC Patterson

Puts us on a
Race making track

The intellegensia has failed to limit us
Nationalism is an irationalism

The intellegensia has failed to limit us
Rise from dust to consciousness

The intellegensia has failed to limit us

Rise from dust to consciousness

Rise from dust to consciousness

Rise,

Rise from dust to consciousness

Part 2
Section 3
1

Marxist sociology
Starts with social
Inequalities
Within cities territory
Is unfairly varied
At the expense
Of the poor, these
Characteristics
Are very specific
To capitalistic
Influence
In regards to real estate
The result is struggle
In the appropriation
Of housing as well
As fewer
Goods for the consumer
The state contributes
To urban structuring
Guided by ideals
Controlling services
Merely puppetry
The municipal in the urban
Text is a puppet
To ruling class interests
When people don't go
Outside their social places
These folks tend
To concentrate this

Is called
Social homo-geniality
Some self-segregate
Due to wealth
In lesser
Cases a menace seems
To stigmatize
Inhabitants
With a malignancy
Referenced
In Wilsons own
With ethnic tones
In areas of low prestige
The exclusion leads
To a vicious
Cycle with no conclusion
No rest

Conviction to spit Marxism like Jameson
Language games from men
Ain't the same, some lived the plot

De-facto is where the facts stroll

Conviction to spit Marxism like Jameson
Language games from men
Ain't the same, some lived the plot
The clot of de-jure segregation
Was stopped

De-facto is where the facts stroll

Dogma

Conviction to spit Marxism like Jameson
Language games from men
Ain't the same, some lived the plot

De-facto is where the facts stroll

2

Segregation produces
Opportunities for the elite
And blocks access to resources
From lower classes moving
Them into poverty and defeat
Through the study
Of segregation residences
We can come closer to understanding
Social spacial processes
In the structuring of cities
And urban social mechanisms depending
On class the neighborhood effect may increase
Or block opportunities
Based on access the approach should be
Typological where variables
Are a like, so obstacles
Posed by certain indexes are closed
And not disturbing the method

Segregation is separation
Based on sex texts or race men
Believe classes
Should be packed in with
Those who look and act like them its
Also economic
Racial flights left men jobless
Generations left in place based plots since
The doctrines
Of politicians who dealt with a problem

Dogma

Through the ideology of presentism
Groups cut off from resources develop truths
steeped in
A demeaned culture born in
The national values the segregated mind is
Warped its right and wrong is trapped in
Those foul views
That never allowed you
To better your house

Conviction to spit Marxism like Jameson
Language games from men
Ain't the same, some lived the plot

De-facto is where the facts stroll

Conviction to spit Marxism like Jameson
Language games from men
Ain't the same, some lived the plot
The clot of de-jure segregation
Was stopped

De-facto is where the facts stroll

Conviction to spit Marxism like Jameson
Language games from men
Ain't the same, some lived the plot

De-facto is where the facts stroll

Part 2
Section 4
1

Through pressure
The creditor gets pleasure
Once a coward
I get my power
From torturing the powerless
The powers absorbing their torment
I gain rank by pulling teeth
No cruelty no feast
Christians had seen in suffering
Salvations machinery other beings
Man has seen in relation to suffering
Have been seen as instigators this blatant
Look at human nature
Was investigated by the Greeks
Life is suffering
The utter bleak suffering
Of an innocent man is evil
Becomes justified if noticed by a deity
Taking pleasure in it then it becomes conceivable, you
Owe them your existence
The cruel spectors
Have your eternal debt on a wish list
I seek to be a buyer
Definitions of piety will change when
I transform society
In my course flows
Rivers of corpses
The divorce of the present

Dogma

For better worlds men who feel guilt
Or the call-to-care are not higher men

Is he higher man or criminal
Through the fire with pliers and an axe
He rips in you
Over rivers of corpses
Not hindered by torment

No cruelty, no feast

Is he higher man or criminal
Through the fire with pliers and an axe
He rips in you
Over rivers of corpses
Not hindered by torment

No cruelty, no feast

No cruelty, no feast

2

People make choices
To heed those same voices
From themselves the law
Or other social noises
Jaws moist poised
To be anointed
With rewards
In the war for needs
Something that leads
One to satisfy a need
Is a reinforcer
Can be primary like appetite
Or secondary like a yearning to write
Our learning is place based
On our conditioning
It came straight
From our past living
The way we were raised
The right and wrong is determined
By the power structure
Might is all turned into law
That flowers in utterly
Every crawl space when punishment
Becomes rubbish
Without delay
It's as if the law was lifted away
Men desire an equitable allocation
Comparing not just gains to gains
But ratio in rectitude of that attained
In the mind of an aggressor
The target the lesser

Dogma

Is far from a victim
It's a sucker deserving a licking
Laboratory settings extrapolated
In a real world dressing has led to a confirmation
Of the theory indicated

Is he higher man or criminal?
Through the fire with pliers and an axe
He rips in you
Over rivers of corpses
Not hindered by torment

No cruelty, no feast

Is he higher man or criminal?
Through the fire with pliers and an axe
He rips in you
Over rivers of corpses
Not hindered by torment

No cruelty, no feast

No cruelty, no feast

3

There is a connection
Between crime
And impulsiveness
With a link to low intelligence
Children raised where aggressiveness
Was relished will have
Internalized inhibitions
Directed toward
Certain penchants
Subcultural values influence decisions
The market in the form
Of mass media has tentacles
That feed dreams
Of freed demons
Schools like prisons bring
The creators of rules together to sit with
Each other and pool mal-contentments

Is he higher man or criminal?

Eidetic
Part 3
Section 1
1

During the first half of the 20th century
There were black communities
With stern class continuities
Supporting moral structures,
Countering abhorrent ruptures
The upper class and middle classes
Could afford decent housing
With the migration of southern blacks
To northern cities feeling that the other lacks
White elites patterned black movements
To cities they strengthened the covenant
To maintain stability using subsidies
From the government
And insurance schemes
Whites kept the suburbs free of diversity
This is a science and an art
To deeply mark men
Contracts by landowners persisted
Under the guise of the free market
Lyndon Baynes Johnson
With his great doctrine
Ended the dejure although it still persisted
He did this to change blocks with
Nothing but starving youths who
Had to work hard for rubbish or rob men
He came from on high to free
Kids to run through the fields of the great society
Imagine a congressionally backed housing bill,

Blacks move in ethnically patterned patterns now unsealed
Middle income blacks exit the citadel
Moving next to whites
Reluctant to live with well next to the blight
Middle income whites stay, it's the
Lower class blacks
Who push out lower class whites in out migration
With the loss of the middle, the inner city
And the white drained s
Suburbs suffers alienation
Unemployment and poor education

Brownish Casual shoes
Boundless mackerel views
Of how this towns sickness
Came about, witness

Brownish Casual shoes
Boundless mackerel views
Of how this towns sickness
Came about, witness
Testimonies

Brownish Casual shoes
Boundless mackerel views
Of how this towns sickness
Came about, witness

Dogma

2
Black leaders traded Millcreek for Pruitt Igo,
You can still see
Civic Progresses will, to leave
Or obtain a residence
For the disadvantage concentrated
Due to negligence
Was impossible and due
To a lack of funds, the prodigals
Left us in a loop that seems illogical
To the outside viewing in
To watch those adaptations to conditions
That zap patience as you enter,
The center, the ruins of stores
And the accruing of moors
Due to a lack of resources
The tragic rides the backs of the poor kids
Who dwell in the scorched city
Marked dark by social movements
The far north has art forms
Documented by global newsmen
Delmar locked you in
Souls grown boxed in crude laws,
Left fumes lost
In patterns caught in
A splatter of race you smell
What's the matter
The bourgeois moved
Now all is bleak, truth
Is an honest thief
It haunts the policies
Of those who fought wrong, you see
The greatest wrong is to leave

RC Patterson

Surplus words must turn the
Sentence into clauses
As I mention men who thought of
The systems I use in urban prognostics
Suburban sins caught us
Mold behind bricks rots lungs
Cancerous, minds sick, tots run
Into traffic as minds bend the plots done
Life is writing
Themes seem timeless
Til we forget

Brownish Casual shoes
Boundless mackerel views
Of how this towns sickness
Came about, witness

Brownish Casual shoes
Boundless mackerel views
Of how this towns sickness
Came about, witness
Testimonies

Brownish Casual shoes
Boundless mackerel views
Of how this towns sickness
Came about, witness

Dogma

Part 3
Section 2
1

The memory trace
In its assembly is similar
To the topic of James
It's the noematic kernel
All that remains
When all else has faded
The experience is inferred no
Constructed socially
And biologically a combination
Even estrogen has been demonstrated
To enhance synaptic plasticity
In the hippocampus
Due to elongated potency
Of the synapse following brief
Synaptic activity
Thus we learn as we experience actively
The world is not just a product
It is constructed
Knowledge is an adaptive function
The real world outside me exists
But how I understand it is constructivist
Dependent on circumstances
Meaning is a property of social behavior
The topic deep in the sentence logic in order
To discover what doesn't change
I used my imagination
To dream up an eidetic variation
If you thought this was a Caucus Room
Approach them you've been tricked

RC Patterson

I'm more open, to truth

How I understand it is constructivist
I used my imagination
To dream up an eidetic variation

How I understand it is constructivist
I used my imagination
To dream up an eidetic variation

How I understand it is constructivist

Dogma

2

Essential insight
In this life
Leaves for mental ties
To the policy past
It's those binds that
Keep calling me back
To sinful times
Where if one were to be black
That person
Who still is cursed lives in
An all-black power structure
Where values are peacefully constructed
Through local initiatives
That connects new global traditions
In a publically facilitated capitalist system
Severe inequality is banished
Free healthcare not only for the tragic
But everyone else as well where do
We start with the creation of values
The cremation of prejudice
Through a bisection and sound use
Of business capital…..etc.
The taxes will fund schools
And strong families, but what of you
What are your ideas?
………………………..

Made in the USA
Charleston, SC
26 June 2013